GLASGOW THEN AND NOW

RUDOLPH KENNA

Contemporary photographs by Alan Dimmick and Duncan I. McEwan

Fort Publishing Ltd

First published in 2001 by Fort Publishing Ltd,
Old Belmont House, 12 Robsland Avenue, Ayr, KA7 2RW

This revised edition published 2005

Printed by Cromwell Press, Trowbridge, Wiltshire, BA14 0XB

ISBN: 0-9547431-4-8

Front cover: George Square, looking north, *c.* 1890

Back Cover: George Square, looking north, 2005

Rudolph Kenna has written extensively about his native city.
His previous publications include *Glasgow Art Deco, The Glasgow Pub Companion, Old Glasgow Streets, Old Glasgow Shops* and *Heart of the Gorbals.*

Alan Dimmick (2001 photographs) and **Duncan McEwan** (2005 photographs) are freelance photographers living and working in Scotland.

Contents

Introduction

Scotland's largest city is no urban parvenu. In the sixth century, there was a religious community in the environs of Glasgow. Evidence of much earlier human activity in the dear green place was uncovered in the eighteenth and early nineteenth centuries. Workmen digging foundations in various parts of the city unearthed no fewer than seventeen prehistoric log boats, one of which contained a Neolithic axe head.

The town was a bishop's burgh by the twelfth century and a royal burgh by 1611. But until fairly recently, chance was far from kind to the built environment. Catastrophic 'great fires', railways and slum clearance schemes, urban motorways and draconian comprehensive development, all took a heavy toll. Time and again Glasgow has been obliged to reinvent itself: university and cathedral town; international tobacco entrepôt; textile town; world capital of shipbuilding and engineering; post-industrial 'European City of Culture' and tourist trap.

By the fifteenth century, Glasgow stretched north from Bishop William Rae's stone bridge at the Stockwell to the cathedral and Bishop's Castle at the top of the High Street. High Street was for centuries the spine of Glasgow, joining 'upper' and 'lower' towns. Bishop John Leslie described Glasgow as it appeared in the late sixteenth century: 'A noble town with a fair situation and pleasant, abundant in garden herbs, apple trees and orchards.'

Until the Reformation, the most important streets – Drygate, Rottenrow, Kirkgate – were in the ecclesiastical upper town or 'townhead'. Merchants and traders lived in the lower town, where an alternative, secular town centre was taking shape. The ecclesiastical part of town stretched almost to present-day Glasgow Cross, for the Dominicans and Franciscans both had convents on High Street. Since by the fifteenth century High Street was also the home of the University, it linked the Glasgow of clerics and academics with the town of merchants, craftsmen and traders.

After the Reformation, the upper town dwindled in importance and the Bishop's Castle fell into ruins. Of the well-built manses and houses which once clustered about the cathedral and castle, and gave distinction to the town head, Provand's Lordship (1471) is the sole survivor.

The new, mercantile town centre was roughly cruciform. Two arms of the cross were Trongate, running west, and Gallowgate, running east; the others were Saltmarket, running south, and High Street, running north. Bridgegate joined the foot of the Saltmarket to the old Glasgow Bridge at the Stockwell. Traveller John Rae admired the town in 1661: 'Fair, large, and well-built, cross-wise, somewhat like unto Oxford, the streets very broad and pleasant.'

Glasgow Cross, the meeting point of the four principal streets, was the centre of urban gravity by the seventeenth century, its status enhanced in 1627 by the erection on the north side of Trongate of a fine new Tolbooth – a combination of town hall, courthouse and jail.

In High Street, Gallowgate and other main thoroughfares, the houses had timber fronts and thatched roofs. In the summer of 1601 a 'great fire' destroyed a portion of the town. Another 'great fire' – the most disastrous in Glasgow's annals – occurred in the summer of 1652. A third of the town went up in flames and around one thousand families lost their homes. A third conflagration, in 1677, left about seven hundred people homeless. After that 'great fire', the town council prohibited the erection of wooden buildings, and by the early eighteenth century, the town's main streets were fronted by substantial stone tenements with crow-stepped gables and colonnaded walks, the famous piazzas. In 1725 an English visitor, Edward Burt, described Glasgow as 'The prettiest and most uniform town that ever I saw.'

As late as 1736, Glasgow was reportedly 'surrounded with cornfields, kitchen and flower gardens, and beautiful orchards, abounding with fruits of all sorts, which by reason of the open and large streets, send forth a pleasant and odoriferous smell'. In 1750 Stockwell Street, where the Trongate ended, was Glasgow's western extremity. A century later, rural villages such as Anderston and Finnieston had been incorporated within the city boundaries.

By the mid seventeenth century, Saltmarket was an exclusive address, home to entrepreneurs such as Walter Gibson, whose town house stood 'upon eighteen stately pillars or arches'. In the 1850s, American novelist Nathaniel Hawthorn saw a very different Saltmarket, where ragged barefooted children appeared to 'have been unwashed from birth'. The once-fashionable heart of Glasgow was by then tightly packed with destitute people from 'John Bull's other island'.

By the middle of the eighteenth century, Virginia merchants, known locally as 'tobacco lords', were building elegant villas to the west of Glasgow Cross. With their classical pediments, ornamental stone urns and gilded window frames, the Palladian houses of the rich merchants made a big impression on visitors.

The east end of Trongate was the merchants' promenade. Decked out in bushy wigs, three-cornered hats and scarlet cloaks, the tobacco lords took sole possession of the 'plainstanes' – an exclusive stretch of pavement west of Glasgow Cross.

By the early 1800s, George Square, consisting of terraced houses, was the best address in town. By 1819 the square, enclosed by railings, boasted a solitary statue – that of Glasgow-born soldier Sir John Moore. The Victorians added a dozen more and removed the railings, turning the square into an open-air sculpture gallery, which they pompously referred to as 'Glasgow's Valhalla'. By the mid nineteenth century the railway had invaded Glasgow. Queen Street station had been built, and the city's hotel world was centred on George Square. Before George Square sprouted hotels such as the Waverley, Crow, Clarence, Globe, Imperial and Royal, travellers put up at two famous hostelries in Argyle Street – the Black Bull Inn and the Buck's Head Hotel.

Other prestigious building developments followed. In the early nineteenth century, entrepreneur Robert Harley established a public 'pleasure garden' on Blythswood Hill. By the 1840s Harley's garden had been replaced by Blythswood Square. But business and commerce soon began to lay siege to the exclusive Blythswood estate. By the 1870s, prosperous citizens were moving further west, to the Olympian seclusion of Woodlands Hill.

Like their eighteenth-century counterparts, nineteenth-century visitors continued to admire Glasgow's townscape. In 1857 Nathaniel Hawthorn wrote: 'I am inclined to think [Glasgow] the stateliest city I ever beheld.' While some visitors were impressed by the crescents, squares and terraces of the West End, others who ventured east and north were overawed by forests of factory chimneys belching great plumes of smoke. A few farsighted individuals protested at the ensuing atmospheric pollution. In 1881 James Burn Russell, Glasgow's crusading Medical Officer of Health, commented that the city had the purest water, but the foulest air, in the United Kingdom.

If the Victorians largely ignored smoke pollution, they at any rate embarked upon slum clearance. Between 1866 and the 1914–18 war, the municipally-controlled City Improvement Trust removed at least 16,000 dwellings in the historic heart of Glasgow. Since the city fathers, with remarkable *sang-froid*, swept away virtually every vestige of Glasgow's past, it would be fair to suggest that they really did throw the baby out with the bath water.

After the Second World War, city planners were even more ambitious than their Victorian predecessors. Glasgow was to be transformed into 'the most modern city in Europe', a radial metropolis of concrete towers and flyovers – with rooftop heli-pads. An incredible twenty-nine comprehensive development areas (CDAs) were proposed, only nine of which had been approved by 1980, by which time attitudes had changed and 'heritage' was firmly on the agenda.

With comprehensive development, tight-knit inner-city communities were rehoused in tower blocks or dispersed to vast peripheral estates and new towns such as East Kilbride and Cumbernauld. By the end of the years of upheaval, Glasgow had decanted some 200,000 people, about one-fifth of the population.

Three concentric ring-roads were planned in the days when motorway engineers were lords of the universe. If the full programme had gone ahead, much of the city would have been levelled. The completed north and west flanks of the M8 went through some of the city's poorest neighbourhoods, adding to the chaos caused by comprehensive development.

In the 1990s the city began to raze tower blocks, and the Red Road flats (1966–70), the highest in Europe, are earmarked for demolition in the near future.

Early views of Glasgow usually featured one or more key buildings, such as the Cathedral, the Tolbooth and the Tron Kirk. Time-travelling Georgians could still get their bearings from these landmarks. And Victorians would recognise much of the built environment they knew. For over-enthusiastic post-war planners did not have it all their own way, and much of the inner-city escaped destruction to become a major tourist attraction at the beginning of the twenty-first century. Wise conservation policies – pioneered by a small minority of percipient citizens – ensured that magnificent buildings survived the iconoclastic years to be given a new lease of life as museums, restaurants, hotels, pubs and upmarket housing.

Glasgow continues to lose irreplaceable listed buildings through fires. The most recent, and tragic, loss was the former Elgin Place church (1856) in Bath Street, a neo-classical master-piece which was hastily demolished after a fire in 2004. But it's not all bad news. Some priceless assets have been restored to their former glory, including the magnificent Doulton fountain on Glasgow Green, the largest terracotta fountain in the world.

Tourism is now a pillar of the local economy. But prosperity is patchy and, as in many other post-industrial cities, it remains to be seen if the latest optimistic reinvention of Glasgow – one of many such hopeful transformations in 700 years – will help bridge the perennial gap between rich and poor in the city.

Rudolph Kenna, 2005

Glasgow from the Fir Park, late seventeenth century.
Beyond the cathedral is the Bishop's Castle. The college or university can be seen in the distance (left of picture) in this view, looking west. The Fir Park was a place of recreation for the city's mercantile families.

Glasgow from the Necropolis, 2001.
The Fir Park became the Necropolis, the merchants' exclusive burial ground, in 1833.
The modern view west takes in the campus of the University of Strathclyde beyond Castle
Street. The site of the Bishop's Castle has vanished beneath the cathedral precinct.

View across river to Clyde Street, *c.* 1820.

The town hospital and poorhouse (1733) is on the right. In the centre of this view north stands St Andrew's RC chapel, completed in 1817. The river Clyde was so shallow at this point that carters could water their horses.

View across river to Clyde Street, 2001.
The chapel, now St Andrew's Roman Catholic cathedral, has acquired a glass-fronted extension housing the Archdiocese of Glasgow.

High Street, looking south, 1828.
This part of the old town was dominated by the seventeenth-century facade of the College (University) of Glasgow, demolished in 1870 and replaced by a railway goods station.

High Street, looking south, 2001.
The College goods station has gone and this long-neglected section of historic High Street awaits redevelopment.

Queen Street, looking west, early nineteenth century.
On the left is the Royal Bank of Scotland, formerly the town mansion of Virginia tobacco merchant William Cunninghame. On the right, the pillared building is the Theatre Royal. Opened in 1805, it was destroyed by fire in 1829.

Queen Street, looking west, 2001.
The Cunninghame mansion was later incorporated in the Royal Exchange (1832), now the Gallery of Modern Art. The equestrian statue of the Duke of Wellington (1844) was the work of Baron Carlo Marochetti.

Argyle Street, looking north, *c.* 1840.

Opened in 1758, the Black Bull Inn was built for the Glasgow Highland Society. Robert Burns lodged there in 1787 and 1788. After the bard's death, the Black Bull became a venue for Burns anniversary dinners.

Argyle Street, looking north, 2001.
This section of the street has been pedestrianised, and a Marks and Spencer store occupies the site of the famous coaching inn.

East side of Stockwell Street, *c.* **1849.**
The former town house of a prosperous citizen has been turned into a tavern and a gas fitter's workshop. In the seventeenth century many wealthy merchants had houses in the street.

East side of Stockwell Street, 2001.
The street was widened by the Corporation in the 1920s. An extensive range of City Improvement Trust buildings extends over the site of the old town house. Further south, a tunnel-like railway viaduct has been removed and gap sites await redevelopment.

Saltmarket, *c.* 1849.
Victorian artists discovered romance in the old town, finding its rickety timber-fronted buildings 'picturesque'.
In reality the slums were nests of contagion, breeding grounds of typhus and cholera. There were no privies or drains, and the air was rank with dunghills.

Saltmarket, 2001.
Saltmarket, with its filthy fever-ridden closes, was redeveloped by the City Improvement Trust, which pioneered 'model tenements for artisans'. Saltmarket's Victorian tenements were rehabilitated in the late twentieth century.

Argyle Street, 1849.
The Buck's Head hotel, on the south side of the street, was formerly the elegant villa (1757) of tobacco merchant John Murdoch.
Among the prized amenities of the Buck's Head was a stove in the privy!

Argyle Street, 2001.
In 1862 Alexander 'Greek' Thomson erected the Buck's Head warehouse, a pioneering iron-framed structure, on the site of the old hotel. It still stands at the corner of Dunlop Street.

Glasgow Cathedral and environs, looking east, 1850.
The Barony Church on the right was an essay in Georgian 'Gothick'. Robert Adam's original Royal Infirmary (1792) is on the extreme left. A horse-drawn omnibus is plying for hire, and liquid refreshment is being dispensed from a horse-drawn cart.

Cathedral Square, looking east, 2001.
The cathedral environs later became Cathedral Square, which was given a facelift in the early 1990s, with landscaping, statues and a controversial new building, the St Mungo Museum of Religious Life and Art.

High Street, looking west, *c.* 1868.
The tenements with crow-stepped gables (centre) were the last relics of the famous 'piazzas', admired by generations of travellers.

High Street, looking west, 2001.
The City Improvement Trust removed the historic tenements, which had degenerated into flea-ridden lodgings, and later erected this towering range of warehouses.

Main Street, Gorbals, looking north, *c.* 1868.
The street ran south from the old Glasgow Bridge at the Stockwell. The pub (right) was originally a chapel attached to the seventeenth-century tower house of the Elphinstones, a prominent Glasgow family.

Gorbals Street, looking north, 2001.
Main Street was renamed Gorbals Street in 1931. By the 1930s, the Gorbals had become a byword for squalor. Many of the crumbling tenements were rat-infested. Currently the area is undergoing regeneration, and luxury penthouses sell for up to £300,000!

High Street, looking south to Glasgow Cross, early 1870s.
College Street is on the right of the photograph. This deprived part of the Victorian city was honeycombed with brothels and shebeens (unlicensed pubs). Pawnshops were also ubiquitous (left).

High Street, looking south to Glasgow Cross, 2001.
After much demolition, including the wilful destruction in the 1970s of neo-classical buildings designed by James Adam, this section of the street has been redeveloped, with brick housing taking the place of stone tenements.

Trongate, looking east, 1870.
Barefooted women and children and W. & C. Percy's bargain boot-store are incongruous features of this animated scene. By the Victorian period, Trongate, where wealthy 'tobacco lords' had purchased luxuries such as silk and lace, had gone down in the world.

Trongate, looking east, 2005.
Since the first edition of this book was published in 2001, this part of Trongate has undergone refurbishment. A mock-baronial confection, built in 1854 for the City of Glasgow Bank, has been turned into apartments.

Bridgegate, looking east to Saltmarket, *c.* 1870.
By the Victorian era the street, once the best address in town, had fallen on hard times. The stately town houses of the gentry had been turned into lodging houses, rag stores and dram shops.

Bridgegate, looking east, 2001.
The Victorian railway cut a swathe through the area. Today Shipbank Lane, leading from Bridgegate to Clyde Street, houses Paddy's Market, a comprehensive flea market.

East side of St Enoch Square, early 1880s.
In its heyday the St Enoch Station hotel (1880), with 200 bedrooms, was the third largest in Europe. The all-male gathering (right) could be heading for a horse-racing event, since 'field glasses' are available for hire.

East side of St Enoch Square, 2001.
Despite a public outcry, the grand Victorian hotel was demolished in the 1970s and the steel-and-glass St Enoch's Centre, consisting of a massive shopping mall crammed with chain stores, was built on the site.

Buchanan Street, looking south, early 1880s.
Oysters were the speciality of the Midland Refreshment rooms (extreme right). The spire of St Enoch's church, demolished in 1925, can be seen in the distance.

Buchanan Street, looking south, 2001.
The north end of Buchanan Street has been transformed by the presence of the Buchanan Galleries, a giant shopping mall. The Waverley Temperance hotel is now the Buchanan hotel.

ARGYLE STREET, GLASGOW, LOOKING W.   11.304. G.W.W.

Argyle Street, looking west, *c.* 1888.
Miller Street is on the right of the picture; Dunlop Street, with the Union hotel, is on the left. The flagstaffs of John Anderson's Royal Polytechnic, a famous Victorian department store, are visible on the south side of the street.

Argyle Street, looking west, 2001.
In 1933 Lewis's (now Debenham's) department store was built on the site of Anderson's Royal Polytechnic. Weary shoppers have taken the place of heavy Victorian vehicular traffic.

Jamaica Street, looking north, *c.* 1888.
With its iron-framed warehouses and heavy traffic, the Victorian street was reminiscent of New York. Its attractions included Walter Wilson's Grand Colosseum, an early department store, resplendent with customised gas lamps.

Jamaica Street, looking north, 2001.
Now a one-way street, Jamaica Street has lost its former bustling character. The Grand Colosseum has gone, but a magnificent early iron-framed warehouse (centre) has been given a new lease of life as the Crystal Palace pub.

Queen Street, seen from Royal Exchange Place, _c._ 1890.
A 'growler' (hackney cab) stands ready for hire. The British Linen Bank on the north side of Ingram Street faces Arthur & Company's wholesale warehouse, an imposing Francophile block in the elaborate style of the Second Empire.

Queen Street, seen from Royal Exchange Place, 2001.
In 1972 the British Linen Bank was replaced by a prime example of Brutalist architecture, the Bank of Scotland. Arthur & Company's warehouse was rebuilt in the late 1940s after the original building was destroyed by a wartime bomb.

SAUCHIEHALL STREET, GLASGOW LOOKING W. 11,305. G.W.W.

Sauchiehall Street, looking west from West Nile Street, 1890s.
Lined with elegant shops, Sauchiehall Street was the favourite promenade of the young and fashionable by the closing years of the nineteenth century. Copland and Lye's department store, the Caledonian House, opened in 1878, can be seen in the distance (left of picture).

Sauchiehall Street, looking west from West Nile Street, 2001.
Watt Brothers (left) is the last of Sauchiehall Street's traditional department stores. A magnificent late-Victorian warehouse (centre right) is now a general market called the Savoy Centre.

Renfield Street, looking north from St Vincent Street, early 1890s.
The youth in the foreground is riding a trace-horse – used to help heavily laden horse-drawn carts up the steep incline to Buchanan Street goods station. Trace-boys and their horses were a familiar sight until the Second World War.

Renfield Street, looking north from St Vincent Street, 2001.
The street retains much of its nineteenth-century character, though Victorian commercial blocks later had to vie for attention with American-style banks, several of which now function as pubs and restaurants.

St Vincent Place, looking east, late 1890s.
A policeman is on traffic duty at the busy junction with Buchanan Street. The ornate lamp standard (right of centre) marks the entrance to Glasgow's first fully-equipped gents' public lavatory, opened in 1892.

St Vincent Place, looking east, 2001.
By the Edwardian period the concentration of sumptuous commercial buildings in this central location had been completed with the Scottish Provident Institute Building and the Anchor Line building. Several of the grand commercial palaces now house pubs and restaurants.

Castle Street, looking north, 1899.
The early electric tram is bound for the south side. The city fathers, being thrifty as well as progressive, recycled 120 horse trams by converting them to electric traction. Glasgow's tramway system was fully electrified by 1901.

Castle Street, looking north, 2001.
The approach to Cathedral Square is now dominated by a mock-medieval castle housing the St Mungo Museum of Religious Life and Art.

St George's Cross, looking west, *c.* 1900.
A Maryhill-bound open-top electric tram is prominent in this view, looking towards Clarendon Place. Another tram, bound for Maryhill barracks, has turned right into Maryhill Road.

St George's Cross, looking west, 2001.
Clarendon Place with its monumental portico is virtually all that survives of the nineteenth-century townscape, which was sacrificed to the M8.

St Enoch Square, looking north-west, early 1900s.
St Enoch subway station (1896) is on the extreme left. William and John Costigane's Bonanza Warehouse, an early cut-price store, occupies one of the Square's original eighteenth-century buildings.

St Enoch Square, looking north-west, 2001.
St Enoch subway station is now an SPT travel centre. The GAP department store, formerly Arnott's, occupies the site of the Bonanza Warehouse, and the principal landmark to the north is still a corner-domed commercial block, formerly Stewart and Macdonald's.

Sauchiehall Street, looking east to Charing Cross, *c.* 1901.
The Grand hotel (left of picture), opened in 1872, was the premier hotel in the West End. It was described by a contemporary American source as 'one of the finest and best appointed hotels in Europe'.

Sauchiehall Street, looking east to Charing Cross, 2001.
The Grand hotel was demolished in 1968 to make way for the M8 and Fountain House, a dismal office block. The Cameron Memorial Fountain (1896) survives, along with Charing Cross Mansions, an exuberant *fin-de-siècle* tenement.

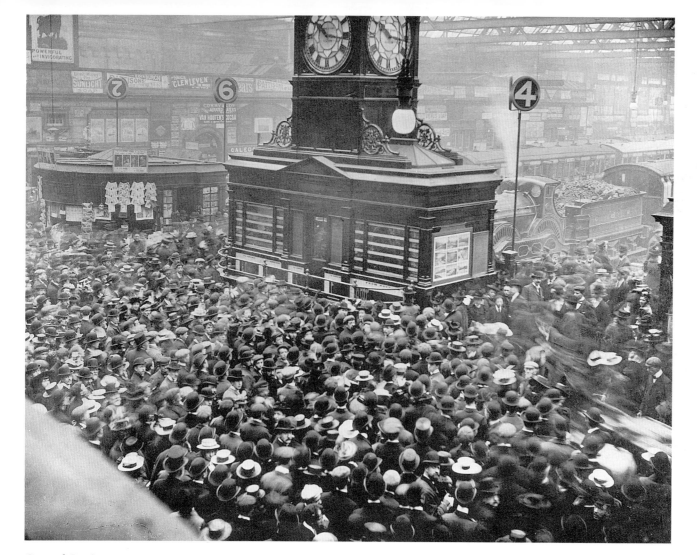

Central Station, *c.* 1900.
The scene was a Glasgow Fair Saturday. Straw hats appear to have been a grudging sartorial concession to the sultry month of July!

Central Station, 2001.
After a £32 million refit the station, originally built for the Caledonian Railway, is one of Europe's most stylish railway terminals. The roof, containing six acres of glass (50,000 panes), has featured in *The Guinness Book of Records*.

Ladywell Street, looking north from Duke Street, early 1900s.
When the photograph was taken, this lime-washed dwelling was the oldest thatched house in Glasgow and was typical of pre-Victorian townscape east of Glasgow Cross.

Ladywell Street, 2001.
A truncated section of the old street survives behind the giant Wellpark Brewery. Ladywell Street originally led north to Glasgow Cathedral and took its name from a public well (right) dedicated to the Virgin Mary.

Trongate, seen from Glasgow Cross, *c.* 1903.
The eighteenth-century Tontine hotel (destroyed by fire in 1912) is on the right. The octagonal-domed building on the left was Glasgow Central Railway's Glasgow Cross station.

Trongate, seen from Glasgow Cross, 2001.

The north side of Trongate was redeveloped by the City Improvement Trust in the 1920s. Glasgow Cross station was demolished in 1977. Its lion-rampart-emblazoned ironwork now adorns a public lavatory in St Vincent Place!

Great Western Road, looking east, 1905.
The lofty spires belong to Lansdowne church and St Mary's Episcopal cathedral.
In the right background is Kelvinbridge subway station.

Great Western Road, looking east, 2001.
Both church spires continue to grace this section of Great Western Road, which has changed little in a hundred years – though the middle of the road is no longer a safe place in which to position lamp standards!

Sauchiehall Street, looking east, 1905.
The Balmoral Temperance hotel is on the extreme left, with Cambridge Street beyond. By the Edwardian era, virtually every novelty, convenience and luxury that money could buy could be obtained in Sauchiehall Street.

Sauchiehall Street, looking east, 2005.
Dunnes Stores (left), a stylish art deco department-store, built in 1929 for C & A Modes, occupies the site of the old hotel.

Govan Road, Govan.

Govan Road, looking west, early 1900s.
The Lyceum music hall (1889) in the background was turned into a cinema in 1923 and destroyed by fire in 1937. It was replaced the following year by a new Lyceum super-cinema on the same site.

Govan Road, looking west, 2001.
The Lyceum cinema is now semi-derelict, but Brechin's Bar still occupies the mock-baronial Cardell Hall, built in 1894 as a centre for temperance workers! Until the removal of industrial grime, the neighbouring statue of shipbuilder Sir William Pearce was known as 'the Black Man'.

Great Western Road, looking west, 1905.
The main entrance to the Botanic Gardens is on the right. The building with gilded onion-shaped domes (1894) was the
Botanic Gardens station of the Glasgow Central Railway.

Great Western Road, looking west, 2001.
When the delightfully eccentric station was destroyed by fire, in 1970, the West End lost a prominent landmark. In Edwardian times, this section of Great Western Road was famous for Sunday afternoon fashion parades!

Reading room in Gorbals library, Main Street, 1907.
Shabbily-dressed men await their turn to peruse newspapers. In inclement weather, the unemployed flocked to the city's public libraries to spend a few hours under shelter.

Gorbals library, 2005.
The old Gorbals library in Main Street, later Gorbals Street, vanished when the area was redeveloped. Equipped with state-of-the-art technology, the new Gorbals library in Crown Street is part of an ambitious urban-regeneration project.

Argyll Arcade, 1908.
Built in 1828 by John Baird, for an entrepreneur called John Reid Robertson, the Parisian-style arcade, linking Argyle Street and Buchanan Street, was Scotland's first enclosed shopping centre.

Argyll Arcade, 2001.
In former times, the L-shaped arcade accommodated all sorts of traders, including milliners, perfumers. opticians, glovers and sheet music dealers. It now functions as Glasgow's jewellery centre.

Dumbarton Road, looking west to Partick Cross, *c.* **1910.**
Byres Road is on the right. By the early 1900s ashlar-fronted tenements had largely replaced the old crow-stepped thatched buildings of Partick, which was absorbed by Glasgow in 1912.

Dumbarton Road, looking west to Partick Cross, 2001.
Substantial tenements still flank this section of Dumbarton Road, which has changed little since the Edwardian era.

Gallowgate, looking east to Belgrove Street and Abercrombie Street, *c.* 1910.
This was the heart of the East End, and a busy traffic intersection, hence the
policeman on points duty. Though imposing in scale, the tenements of this
working-class district left much to be desired in terms of amenities.

Gallowgate, looking east to Belgrove Street and Abercrombie Street, 2005.
The Victorian tenements were swept away in the course of comprehensive development. Population density in this historic part of Glasgow has diminished considerably since the Edwardian era.

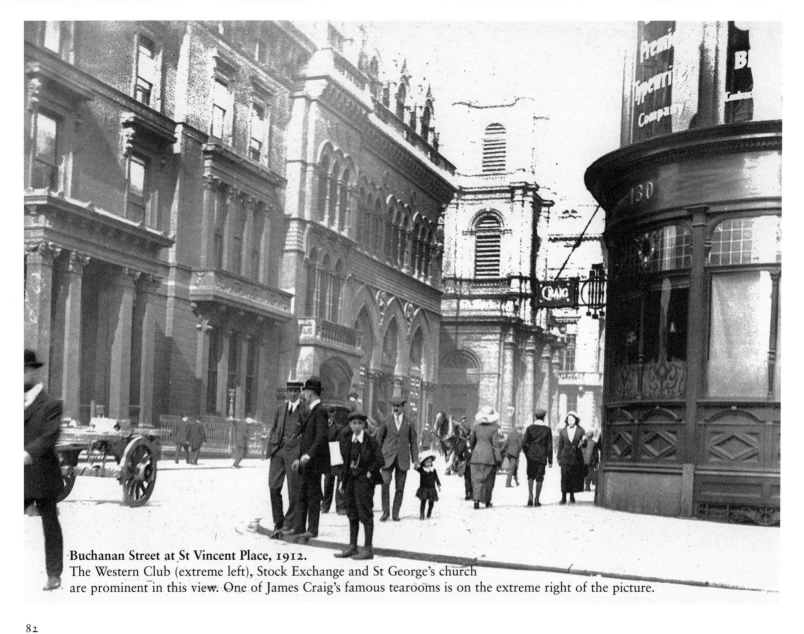

Buchanan Street at St Vincent Place, 1912.
The Western Club (extreme left), Stock Exchange and St George's church
are prominent in this view. One of James Craig's famous tearooms is on the extreme right of the picture.

Buchanan Street at Nelson Mandela Place, 2005.
Nearly a hundred years on, this is still a superb piece of nineteenth-century townscape. Mr Craig's tearoom is now a shop specialising in expensive Scottish knitwear.

Glasgow Bridge, looking south, 1914.
Several photographs were taken on 17 April 1914 at congestion points around the city centre. Motor vehicles, including taxis, are already prominent. The city's electric trams were colour-coded, with red, blue, white, green and yellow bands to indicate the routes.

Glasgow Bridge, looking south, 2005.
At no time of the day is traffic across the bridge as heavy as it was in the Edwardian period, when the new Glasgow Bridge, leading to Jamaica Street, was the main transpontine link, a function now fulfilled by the Kingston bridge.

Glasgow Cross, looking towards Saltmarket, 1916.
The pub offers 'new munitions ale'. During the first world war, to conserve grain and promote efficiency in the munitions and allied industries, ales were less potent than prewar brews.

Glasgow Cross, looking towards Saltmarket, 2001.
The pub survives, renamed the Tolbooth bar. It's still a popular watering hole, though a glass of ale can no longer be obtained for 2*d*!

St Andrew's Cross, looking north-east, 1917.
On the right, belching smoke from twin chimney stacks, is St Andrew's Works, an electricity-generating station, built by Glasgow Corporation in 1900.

St Andrew's Cross, 2001.
St Andrew's Cross, now better known as Eglinton Toll, is a mere shadow of its former self. The old power station has changed its function and lost its chimneys, but the distinctive corner tenement has survived.

Buchanan Street, looking north, 1926.
Trams were not allowed into the city's smartest shopping centre. While other city streets were paved with granite setts, douce Buchanan Street had a smooth surface of tar macadam.

Buchanan Street, looking north, 2001.
Now fully pedestrianised, Buchanan Street still has some of Glasgow's most exclusive shops, including Fraser's (left),
which boasts a magnificent late-Victorian galleried saloon with glazed barrel-vaulted roof.

The Barras market, Calton, *c.* 1926. At the other end of the social spectrum from Buchanan Street was the Barras, in Glasgow's East End, where people on low incomes were able to purchase the bare necessities of existence. In this picture, a trader demonstrates a product called 'the Lightning Cleaner'.

The Barras, 2005.
The famous Barras market is flourishing as never before. Keeping up with the consumer society, it has diversified to offer everything from DVDs to art deco lamps!

East end of Sauchiehall Street, *c.* 1928.
The Empire Palace theatre dominates this view. Opened in 1897 by impresario H. E. Moss, it was demolished in 1963. Because English comedians were given a hard time by discriminating Glasgow audiences, the theatre became known as 'the comics' graveyard'.

Sauchiehall Street, 2005.
Empire House, (centre) a low-rise commercial development, was built in 1964–5 on the site of the famous theatre. Trees are now growing in this part of Sauchiehall Street for the first time in over 150 years!

Photographic credits

The old prints and photographs were drawn from a variety of sources:

Mitchell Library/City Archives, Glasgow: 8, 10, 12, 14, 16, 18, 20, 22, 24, 26, 28, 30, 34, 52, 56, 62, 74, 76, 78, 82, 84, 86, 88

Burrell Gallery, Glasgow: 54, 92

Annan Gallery, Glasgow: 58, 60, 64, 66, 68, 72, 80, 90

Newsquest (*Herald and Evening Times*) Ltd: 94

Author's Collection: 70

George Washington Wilson Collection, University of Aberdeen: front cover, 32, 36, 38, 40, 42, 44, 46, 48, 50